Theory Paper Grade 7   2007   A

Duration 3 hours

Candidates should answer all FIVE questions.
Write your answers on this paper — no others will be accepted.
Answers must be written clearly and neatly — otherwise marks may be lost.

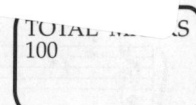
100

1 Indicate suitable chords for a continuo player by figuring the bass as necessary, *from the beginning of bar 4*, at the places marked ∗ in this passage. If you wish to use a ⁵₃ chord, leave the space under the asterisk blank, but ⁵₃ chords *must* be shown as part of a ⁶₄ ⁵₃ progression or when chromatic alteration is required. All other chords should be indicated, as should any suspended dissonances.

15

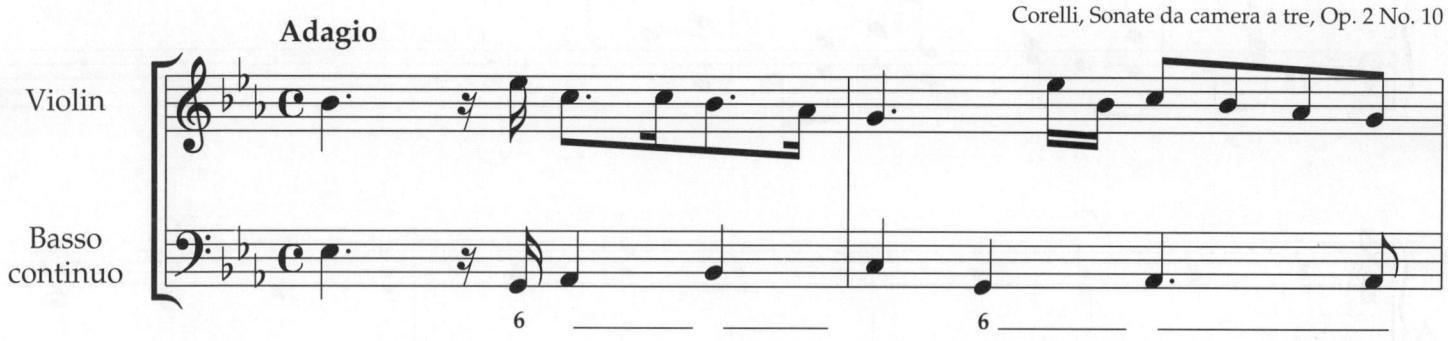

© 2007 by The Associated Board of the Royal Schools of Music

2. On the staves marked **A** below is an outline of part of a chorale harmonized by J. S. Bach, leaving out certain suspensions, passing notes and other notes of melodic decoration. The music on the staves marked **B** is what the composer actually wrote. Continuing in the same style, reconstruct the blank and partially completed bars.

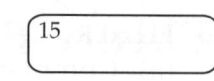

3 EITHER

(a) Complete the flute part in the following passage, which is adapted from a song by Fanny Mendelssohn. Phrase marks have been inserted above the flute stave to indicate the structure you might use.

OR

(b) Compose a complete melody of not less than eight bars in length for unaccompanied cello or trombone, based on the given opening. Include appropriate performance directions for the instrument of your choice and state below which it is.

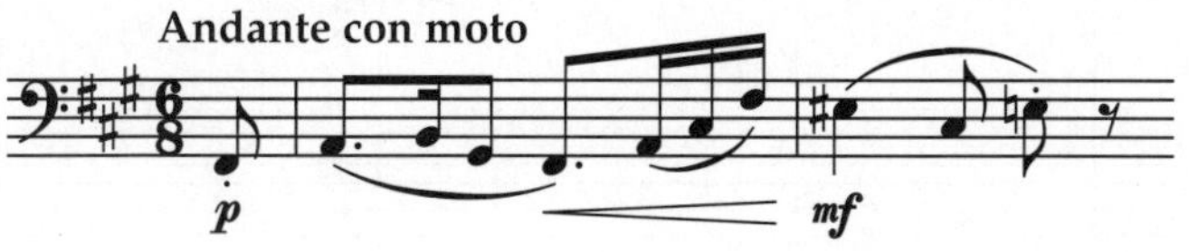

4 Look at the extract printed opposite, which is from a string quartet, and then answer the questions below.   (25)

(a) Complete the following statements:

In bars 7–8 there is a(n) .... cadence in the key of ....

and then the music passes through the key of .... in bar(s) ....   (4)

The music then passes through the key of .... before reaching a perfect

cadence (Ic–V⁷–I) in this key in bar(s) ....   (2)

(b) Write out in full the first violin part of bar 22 as you think it should be played.

   (3)

(c) Identify the chord marked * in bar 21 by writing on the dotted lines below. Use either words or symbols. Indicate the position of the chord, whether it is major, minor, augmented or diminished, and name the prevailing key.

Chord .... Key .... (4)

(d) Mark **clearly** on the score, using the appropriate capital letter for identification, one example of each of the following. Also give the bar number of each of your answers.

A a pair of simultaneous chromatic unaccented passing notes a 3rd apart (circle the notes

    concerned). Bar ....   (2)

B a diminished 7th chord. Bar ....   (2)

C a place where the first violin and viola sound in unison (circle the notes concerned).

    Bar ....   (2)

D the harmonic interval of a compound diminished 4th (diminished 11th) sounding between

    the second violin and cello (circle the notes concerned). Bar ....   (2)

E in bars 21–28, an ascending chromatic semitone. Bar ....   (2)

(e) From the following list, underline the name of the most likely composer of this extract.

    Brahms   Handel   Mozart   Schoenberg   (2)

5 The extract printed on pages 9–10 is from *Ibéria*, which is part of Debussy's orchestral work *Images*. Look at it and then answer the questions below.

(a) Give the meaning of:

Lent .... (1)

unis. (e.g. violas, bar 1) .... (2)

Cédez (bar 3) .... (2)

sourdines (e.g. second violins, bar 3) .... (2)

très doux (bassoon, bar 6) .... (2)

(b) (i) Write out the parts for clarinets in bars 3–5 as they would sound at concert pitch.

(4)

(ii) Using the blank stave on page 10, write out the parts for horns in bars 7–8 as they would sound at concert pitch. (2)

(c) Complete the following statements:

(i) The diagonal lines in the first violin part in bar 8 ( ) indicate that the performers should .... (2)

(ii) A double-reed instrument (not playing in this extract) that has the same interval of transpostion as the horn in F is the .... (2)

(iii) The instrument that *sounds* in unison with the double basses on the first beat of bar 1 is the .... and the instrument that *sounds* in unison with the violas on the first beat of bar 6 is the .... (4)

(iv) The harmonic interval *sounding* between the double basses and cellos on the first beat of bar 2 is a(n) .... (2)

(b) (ii) Horns, bars 7–8

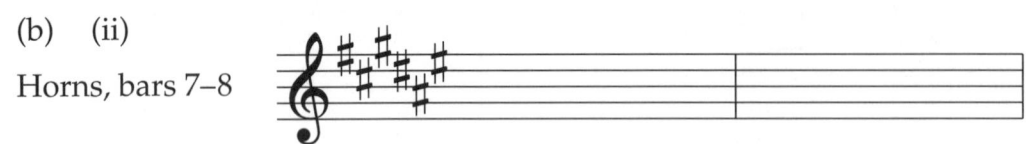

Theory Paper Grade 7 2007 B

Duration 3 hours

Candidates should answer all FIVE questions.
Write your answers on this paper — no others will be accepted.
Answers must be written clearly and neatly — otherwise marks may be lost.

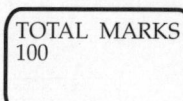

DO NOT
PHOTOCOPY
© MUSIC

TOTAL MARKS
100

1 Indicate suitable chords for a continuo player by figuring the bass as necessary, *from the beginning of bar 4*, at the places marked * in this passage. If you wish to use a $\frac{5}{3}$ chord, leave the space under the asterisk blank, but $\frac{5}{3}$ chords *must* be shown as part of a $\frac{6}{4}\frac{5}{3}$ progression or when chromatic alteration is required. All other chords should be indicated, as should any suspended dissonances.

15

2. On the staves marked **A** below is an outline of part of a chorale harmonized by J. S. Bach, leaving out certain suspensions, passing notes and other notes of melodic decoration. The music on the staves marked **B** is what the composer actually wrote. Continuing in the same style, reconstruct the blank and partially completed bars.

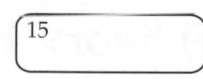

3 **EITHER**

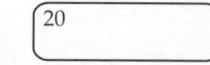

(a) Complete the violin part in the following passage, which is adapted from a piece by Dyson. Phrase marks have been inserted above the violin stave to indicate the structure you might use.

© 1920 Stainer & Bell Ltd, 23 Gruneisen Road, London N3 1DZ
www.stainer.co.uk

OR

(b) Compose a complete melody of not less than eight bars in length for unaccompanied oboe or trumpet (at concert pitch), based on the given opening. Include appropriate performance directions for the instrument of your choice and state below which it is.

Instrument ....

4 Look at the extract from a piano piece, printed opposite, and then answer the questions below. (25)

(a) Give the meaning of **Andante con moto**

   .... (3)

(b) Identify the chord marked ✻ in bar 5 by writing on the dotted lines below. Use either words or symbols. Indicate the position of the chord, whether it is major, minor, augmented or diminished, and name the prevailing key.

   Chord .... Key .... (4)

(c) In bars 1–12, identify the following named cadences by marking them with a bracket (⌐‾‾‾¬) and the appropriate capital letter for identification. Also give the bar number(s) of each of your answers.

   X Imperfect cadence. Bar(s) .... (2)

   Y Perfect cadence. Bar(s) .... (2)

   Z Interrupted cadence. Bar(s) .... (2)

(d) Mark **clearly** on the score, using the appropriate capital letter for identification, one example of each of the following. Also give the bar number(s) of each of your answers.

   A four consecutive melodic notes that form the chord of a *diminished* 7th

   (mark ⌐ A ¬ over the notes concerned). Bar(s) .... (2)

   B four consecutive melodic notes that form the chord of a *dominant* 7th

   (mark ⌐ B ¬ over the notes concerned). Bar(s) .... (2)

   C the harmonic interval of a diminished 5th in the left-hand part. Bar .... (2)

(e) Name three ways in which the composer creates a sense of surprise at bar 21.

   1 .... (1)

   2 .... (1)

   3 .... (1)

(f) From the following list, underline the name of the most likely composer of this extract.

            Haydn   Debussy   Mendelssohn (1)

   Give a reason for *not* choosing each of the other two composers.

   1 .... (1)

   2 .... (1)

5 Look at the extract printed on pages 17–18, which is from Walton's Violin Concerto, and then answer the questions below.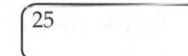

   (a) Give the meaning of:

   a tempo subito .... (2)

   arco (cellos, bar 8) .... (2)

   secco (e.g. first violins, bar 9) .... (2)

   a 2 (flutes, bar 10) .... (2)

   (b) (i) Write out the part for clarinet in bars 1–2 as it would sound at concert pitch.

   (4)

   (ii) The part printed below is played earlier in this concerto by the horn in F. Write it out as it would sound at concert pitch.

   (3)

   (c) Mark **clearly** on the score, using the appropriate capital letter for identification, one example of each of the following. Also give the bar number(s) of each of your answers.

   A a double stop in the part for solo violin. Bar .... (2)

   B a place where the second bassoon *sounds* at the same pitch as the double basses (circle the notes concerned). Bar(s) .... (2)

   C the melodic interval of an augmented 2nd in a part for a double-reed instrument (circle the notes concerned). Bar .... (2)

   D a place where the previously divided cellos are instructed to play the same part together. Bar .... (2)

   E a note and its enharmonic equivalent *sounding* at the same pitch at the same time in the first violin (*not* solo violin) and harp parts (circle the notes concerned). Bar .... (2)

Theory Paper Grade 7 2007 C

Duration 3 hours

Candidates should answer all FIVE questions.
Write your answers on this paper — no others will be accepted.
Answers must be written clearly and neatly — otherwise marks may be lost.

TOTAL MARKS
100

1. Indicate suitable chords for a continuo player by figuring the bass as necessary, *from the beginning of bar 5*, at the places marked * in this passage. If you wish to use a $\substack{5\\3}$ chord, leave the space under the asterisk blank, but $\substack{5\\3}$ chords *must* be shown as part of a $\substack{6\\4}$ $\substack{5\\3}$ progression or when chromatic alteration is required. All other chords should be indicated, as should any suspended dissonances.

15

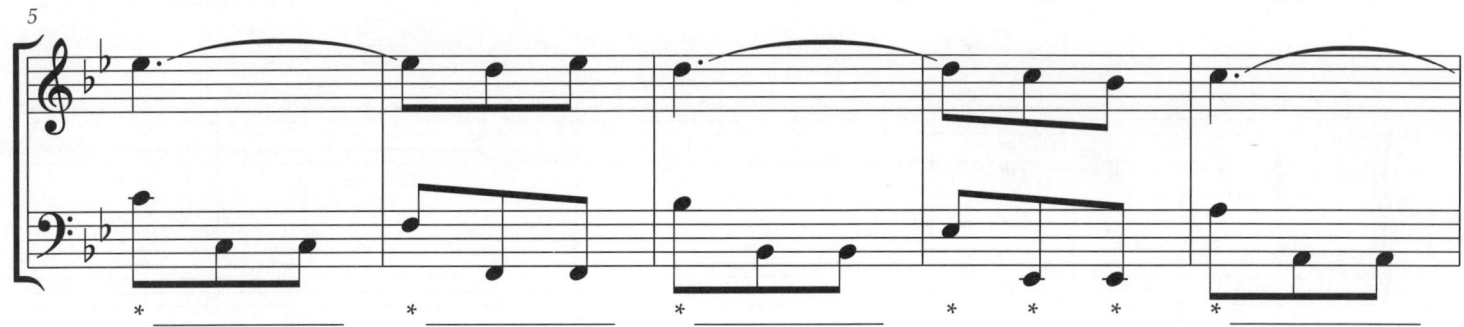

2 On the staves marked **A** below is an outline of a passage adapted from a piano piece by T. Kirchner, leaving out certain passing notes and other notes of melodic decoration. The music on the staves marked **B** is what the composer actually wrote. Continuing in the same style, reconstruct the blank and partially completed bars.

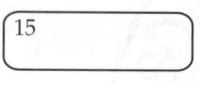

3 **EITHER**
   (a) Complete the flute part in the following passage, which is adapted from a violin piece by Carse. Phrase marks have been inserted above the flute stave to indicate the structure you might use.

© 1919 Stainer & Bell Ltd, 23 Gruneisen Road, London N3 1DZ
www.stainer.co.uk

OR

   (b) Compose a complete melody of eight bars in length for unaccompanied cello or bassoon. Form your melody from the chord progression below, using the chords for each bar, together with any diatonic or chromatic decorations you consider appropriate. You may use the given opening or not, as you prefer. Write the complete melody on the staves below, include appropriate performance directions for the instrument of your choice and state below which it is.

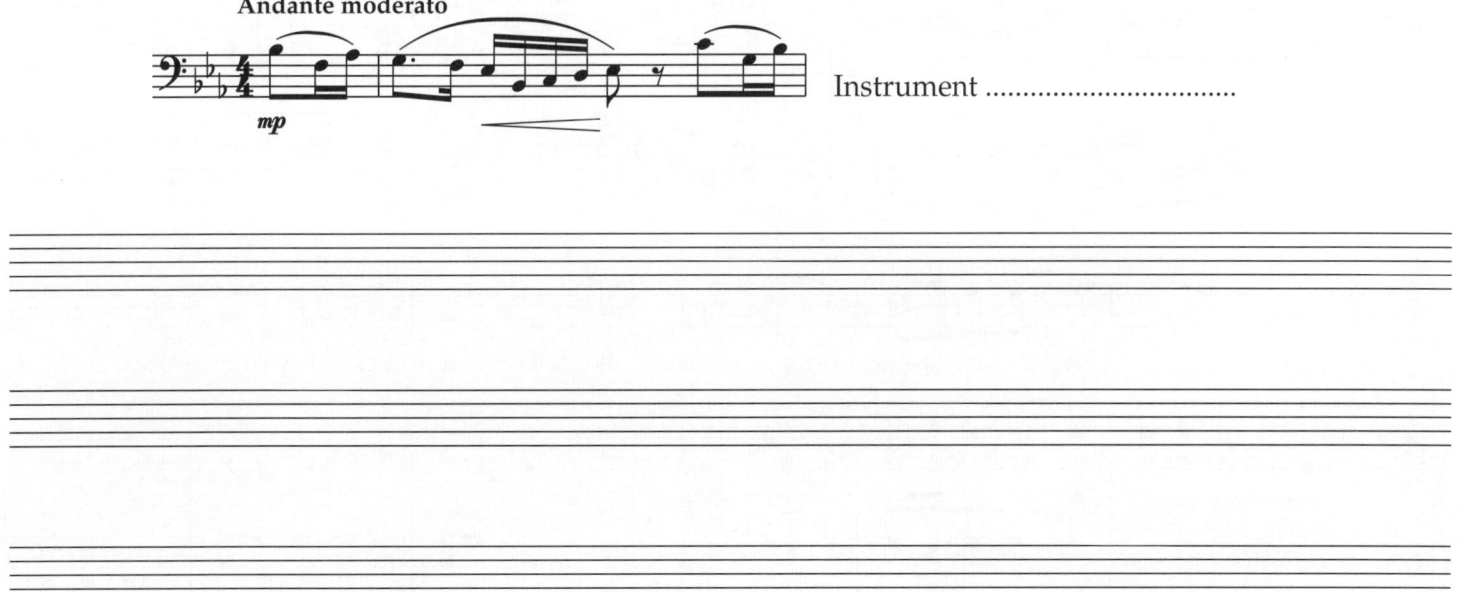

Instrument ....

4 Look at the extract from a song, printed opposite, and then answer the questions below. [25]

(a) Identify the chord marked * in bar 27 by writing on the dotted line below. Use either words or symbols. Indicate the position of the chord and whether it is major, minor, augmented or diminished. The prevailing key is C minor.

Chord .... Key: C minor (3)

(b) Describe fully the numbered and bracketed harmonic intervals in the piano part:

1 bar 5, third beat (right-hand and top left-hand notes) .... (2)

2 bar 21, final quaver (right-hand and bottom left-hand notes) .... (2)

(c) Mark **clearly** on the score, using the appropriate capital letter for identification, one example of each of the following. Also give the bar number(s) of each of your answers.

In bars 1–15

A a diminished 7th chord. Bar .... (2)

B a note of anticipation in the vocal part. Bar .... (2)

In bars 16–31

C two consecutive bars where every note of the right-hand piano part sounds in unison with the vocal part. Bars .... (2)

D the melodic interval of a diminished 3rd in an inner part (circle the notes concerned). Bar .... (2)

E a decorated interrupted cadence in C minor. Bars .... (2)

F two consecutive changing notes in the left-hand piano part (circle the notes concerned). Bar .... (2)

(d) Answer TRUE or FALSE to each of the following statements:

(i) The largest melodic interval in bars 1–24 of the vocal part is a minor 6th. .... (2)

(ii) The top line of the piano part always plays at the same pitch or below that of the singer.

.... (2)

(e) From the following list, underline the name of the most likely composer of this extract, and give a reason for your answer.

    Handel   Schumann   Haydn (1)

Reason:

.... (1)

5 Look at the extract printed on pages 25–26, which is from Prokofiev's *Peter and the Wolf*, and then answer the questions below.

(a) Mark **clearly** on the score, using the appropriate capital letter for identification, one example of each of the following. Also give the bar number(s) of each of your answers.

    A   the harmonic interval of a diminished 7th *sounding* between the double basses and third horn (circle the notes concerned). Bar .... (2)

    B   in bars 10–15, *four* consecutive melodic notes that form a dominant 7th in first inversion in the key of D major (circle the notes concerned). Bar(s) .... (2)

    C   a bar where a wind instrument and a string section play the same written notes but *sound* an octave apart (circle both parts). Bar .... (2)

    D   a double stop that forms the harmonic interval of a major 6th. Bar .... (2)

(b) In this extract the parts for horns and clarinets are printed *at concert pitch*.

    (i) Write out the first and second horn parts in bar 3 for *horns in F* at *written pitch* using the given clef. Do *not* use a key signature.

                                                                                                                                                               (4)

    (ii) Using the blank stave on page 26, write out the clarinet part in bar 12 for *clarinet in B♭* at *written pitch*. (5)

(c) Give the meaning of:

Tamburo militare .... (2)

Piatti .... (2)

𝄎 (e.g. cellos, bar 2) .... (2)

precipitato (clarinet, bar 13) .... (2)

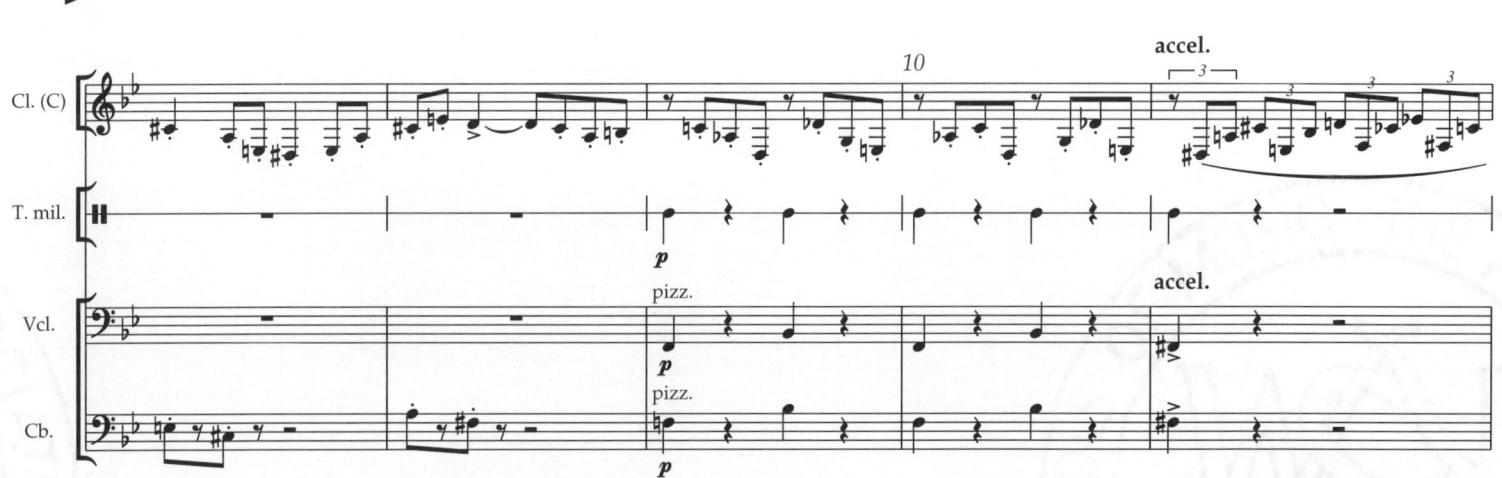

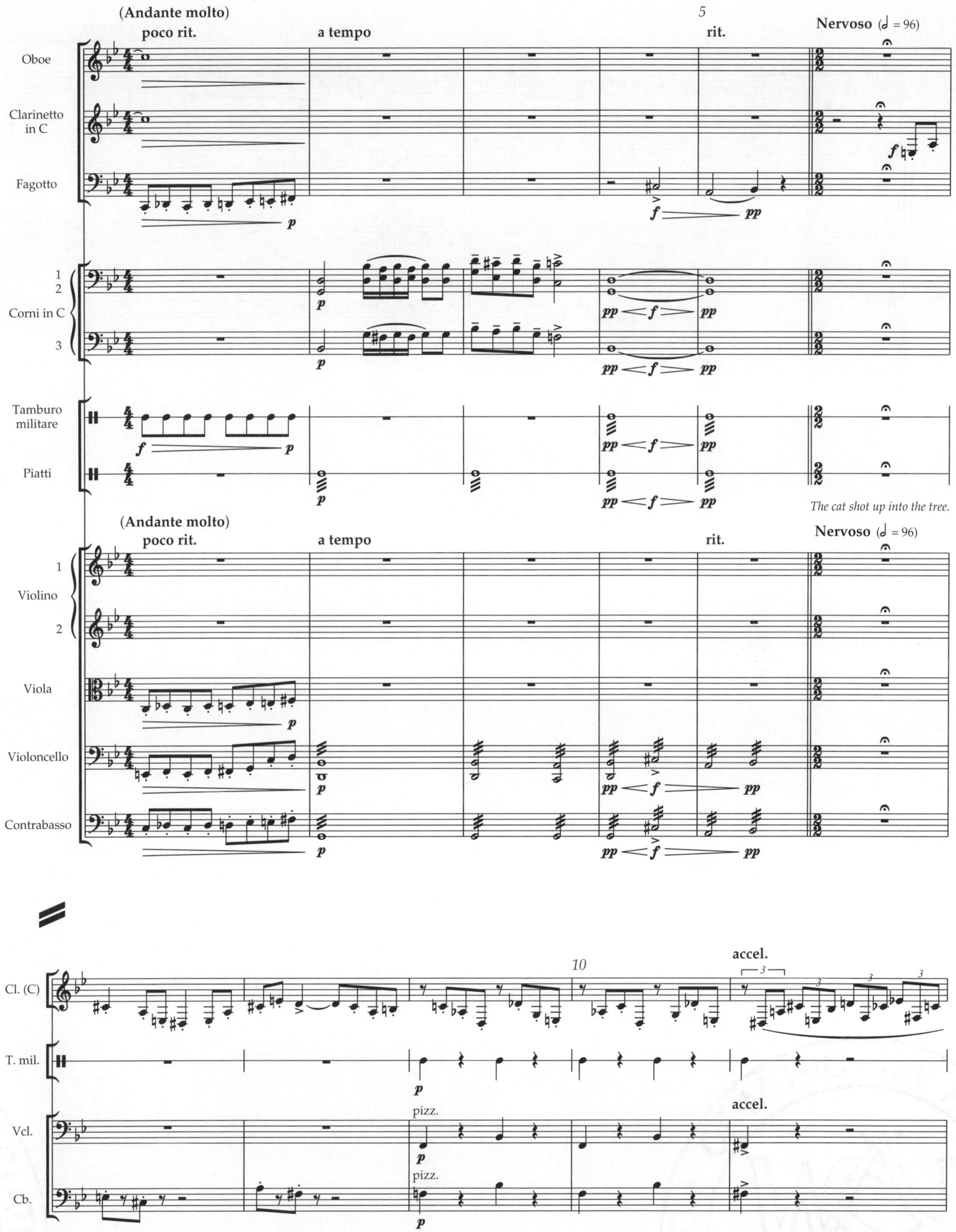
(Andante molto)
poco rit.
a tempo
5
rit.
Nervoso (𝅗𝅥 = 96)
Oboe
Clarinetto in C
Fagotto
Corni in C
Tamburo militare
Piatti
The cat shot up into the tree.
Violino
Viola
Violoncello
Contrabasso
10
accel.
Cl. (C)
T. mil.
Vcl.
Cb.
pizz.

(b) (ii) Clarinet, bar 12

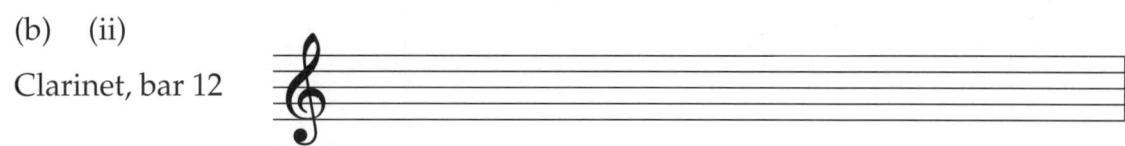

Theory Paper Grade 7 2007 S

DO NOT PHOTOCOPY © MUSIC

Duration 3 hours

Candidates should answer all FIVE questions.
Write your answers on this paper — no others will be accepted.
Answers must be written clearly and neatly — otherwise marks may be lost.

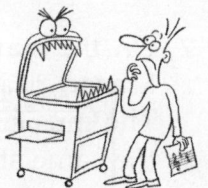

TOTAL MARKS 100

1 Indicate suitable chords for a continuo player by figuring the bass as necessary, *from the third beat of bar 3*, at the places marked * in this passage. If you wish to use a $\substack{5\\3}$ chord, leave the space under the asterisk blank, but $\substack{5\\3}$ chords *must* be shown as part of a $\substack{6\\4}\ \substack{5\\3}$ progression or when chromatic alteration is required. All other chords should be indicated, as should any suspended dissonances.

15

Allegro

Locatelli, Sonata in D minor (adapted)

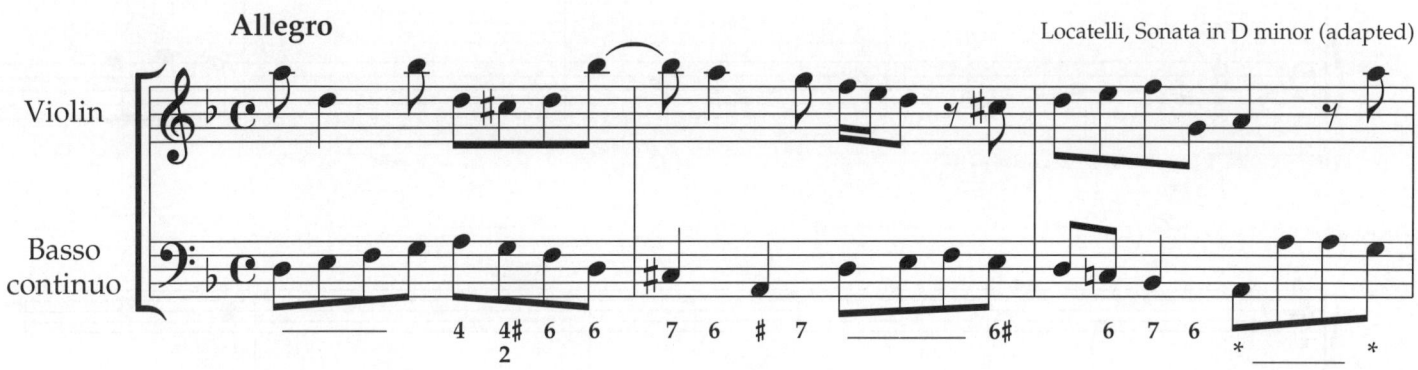

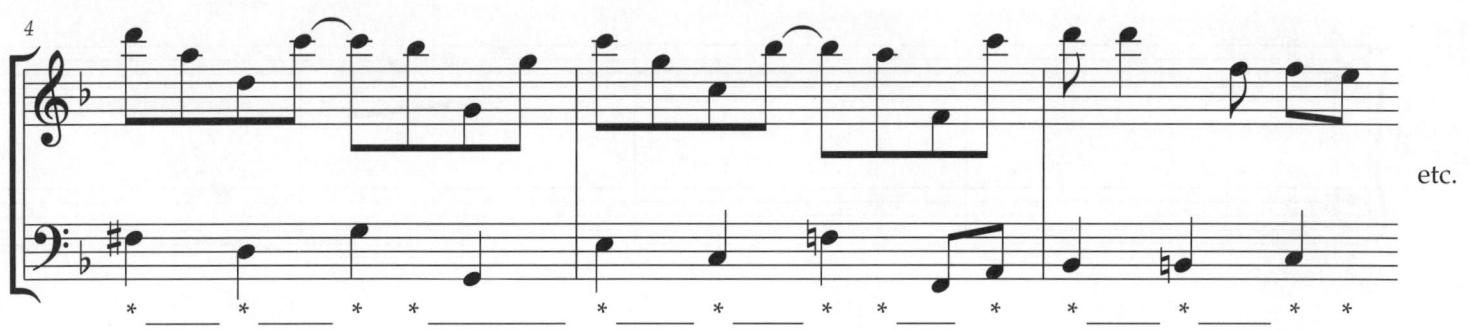

2 On the staves marked **A** below is an outline of a passage adapted from a minuet by Mozart, leaving out certain rests, passing notes and other notes of melodic decoration. The music on the staves marked **B** is what the composer actually wrote. Continuing in the same style, reconstruct the blank and partially completed bars.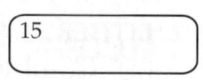

3 EITHER

(a) Complete the violin part in the following passage, which is adapted from a piece by Schumann. Phrase marks have been inserted above the violin stave to indicate the structure you might use.

OR

(b) Compose a complete melody of eight bars in length for unaccompanied flute or violin. Form your melody from the chord progression below, using the chords for each bar, together with any diatonic or chromatic decorations you consider appropriate. You may use the given opening or not, as you prefer. Write the complete melody on the staves below, include appropriate performance directions for the instrument of your choice and state below which it is.

Instrument ....

4 Look at the extract printed opposite, which is from Gilbert and Sullivan's operetta *HMS Pinafore*, and then answer the questions below.

(a) Identify the chord marked ∗ in bar 7 of the piano part by writing on the dotted line below. Use either words or symbols. Indicate the position of the chord and whether it is major, minor, augmented or diminished. The key is E minor.

Chord .... Key: E minor (3)

(b) Mark **clearly** on the score, using the appropriate capital letter for identification, one example of each of the following. Also give the bar number(s) of each of your answers.

    A   a two-bar sequence (not exact) a tone lower than the previous two bars (mark ⌐ A ⌐ over the bars). Bars .... (2)

    B   a modulation to D major. Bar(s) .... (2)

    C   an imperfect cadence in E minor. Bar(s) .... (2)

    D   the melodic interval of a diminished 3rd in the solo part. Bar .... (2)

(c) Give the full name (e.g. note of anticipation) of each of the numbered and circled notes of melodic decoration.

    1 (bar 9, F♯) .... (2)

    2 (bar 17, G♯) .... (2)

    3 (bar 24, F♯) .... (2)

(d) Complete the following statements:

    (i) The interval between the lowest and highest notes of the solo vocal part in the extract is a(n) .... and the harmonic interval between the bass and alto parts in the chorus in bar 15 (bracketed) is a(n) .... (4)

    (ii) The female solo voice category used in this extract has a range between those of the soprano and alto and is called a .... (2)

    (iii) The writing for the chorus is not contrapuntal but more syllabic and chordal and this is called .... (2)

5 Look at the extract printed on pages 33–34, which is from Sibelius's Violin Concerto, and then answer the questions below.

   (a) Give the meaning of:

   tr~~~~ (timpani, bar 4) .... (2)

   B nach H (here 'nach' means 'to') (timpani, bar 6) ....

   .... (2)

   sonoro ed espressivo (solo violin, bar 6) ....

   .... (3)

   (b) Identify the chord marked ∗ in bar 8 by writing on the dotted line below. Use either words or symbols. Indicate the position of the chord and whether it is major, minor, augmented or diminished. The key is B♭ major.

   Chord .... Key: B♭ major (3)

   (c) (i) Write out the parts for clarinets in bar 1 as they would sound at concert pitch.

   (3)

   (ii) Using the blank staves at the foot of page 34, write out the parts for the four horns in bar 10 as they would sound at concert pitch, and using the given clefs. (5)

   (d) Name two ways in which the composer ensures that the solo violin will be heard at its entry in bar 6.

   1 .... (2)

   2 .... (2)

   (e) Complete the following statements:

   (i) In bar 13 the viola plays the ascending scale of .... and in bar 15 the notes that the viola plays can be found in the major scale of .... (2)

   (ii) In bar 10 '2.' in the bassoon part means .... (1)

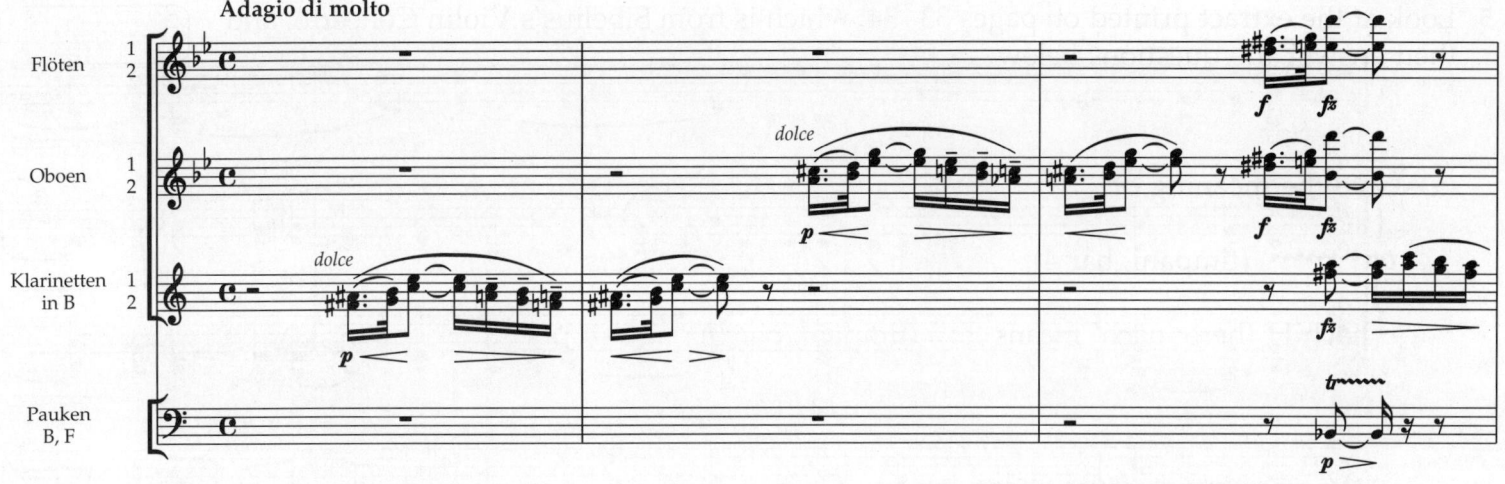

Theory of Music Exams Model Answers, 2007 are now available from your usual retailer.

Grade 1   978-1-86096-882-2
Grade 2   978-1-86096-883-9
Grade 3   978-1-86096-884-6
Grade 4   978-1-86096-885-3
Grade 5   978-1-86096-886-0
Grade 6   978-1-86096-887-7
Grade 7   978-1-86096-888-4
Grade 8   978-1-86096-889-1

Other music theory publications from ABRSM Publishing include:

Theory Workbooks
Grades 6 to 8 (separately)
by Anna Butterworth, Anthony Crossland,
Terence Greaves and Michael Jacques

Music Theory in Practice
Grades 1 to 5 (separately)
by Eric Taylor

Grades 6 to 8 (separately)
by Peter Aston & Julian Webb

The AB Guide to Music Theory
Parts I and II
by Eric Taylor

Harmony in Practice
by Anna Butterworth

ISBN 978-1-86096-878-5

The Associated Board of
the Royal Schools of Music
(Publishing) Limited

24 Portland Place
London W1B 1LU
United Kingdom

www.abrsmpublishing.com